The Nasiri Du'a

THE NASIRI DU'A

by

Shaykh Muhammad – Fatha – ibn Muhammad ibn Ahmad ibn Muhammad ibn al-Husayn ibn Nasir ibn 'Amr ad-Dar'i al-Aghlabi (d. 1085 AH)

translated by

Aisha Bewley

The Nasiri Du'a

Published by: Diwan Press Ltd.
6 Terrace Walk,
Norwich
NR1 3JD
UK
Website: www.diwanpress.com
E-mail: info@diwanpress.com

Author: Shaykh Muhammad ibn Nasir
Translation: Aisha Bewley
Typeset by: Abdassamad Clarke
Cover design by: Abdassamad Clarke
A catalogue record of this book is available from the British Library.

ISBN-13: 978-1-908892-45-4
(paperback)

Printed and bound by: Lightning Source

The Nasiri Supplication

by Shaykh Muhammad - Fatha - ibn Muhammad ibn Ahmad ibn Muhammad ibn al-Husayn ibn Nasir ibn 'Amr ad-Dar'i al-Aghlabi (d. 1085 AH)

Buried in his *zawiya* in Tamagurt.

Introduction

Praise belongs to Allah.

His student, the great scholar Sidi al-Hasan ibn Mas'ud al-Yusi (d. 1102 AH) says about him in *al-Fihrist*:

> He was involved in many areas of knowledge such as *fiqh*, Arabic, *kalam*, *tafsir* and *tasawwuf*. He was a man of worship and of great devotion, scrupulous, and a *zahid*, a man who established the *tariqa* and drank from the source of the Reality. May Allah have mercy on Him - as well as busying himself with the sciences of the people of *tasawwuf* and following the Path, he was not niggardly with outward knowledge regarding teaching, writing, recording and precision. May Allah benefit both groups through him. People from east and west kept his company and posterity benefited through him. He taught his *murids* through word and deed. His *himma* was lofty and his state pleasing. He had sound knowledge and illuminated insight as well as

mastery and self-assurance. When he spoke his words were engraved on people's hearts.

Imam al-Yusi said: "It was reported to me that his teacher, Sidi 'Abdullah Husayn ar-Raqi (d. 1045 AH), who is not the Sidi 'Abdullah ibn Husayn al-Wamghari who is buried in Tamsaluht near Marrakesh, said to the *fuqara'*, 'When the *nafs* of one of you asks for a drink of water, he should let it wait a time, not because there is any harm in drinking water, but so that the *nafs* does not become accustomed to speedy gratification in receiving what it wants.'"

Imam al-Yusi speaks a lot about his shaykh, Imam Ibn Nasir in his books, *al-Muhadarat* and *al-Fihrist*. Al-Yusi was not only concerned with Shaykh Ibn Nasir from the point of view of knowledge, but he was also concerned with him in respect of the science of the *nafs* and what it includes in the way of feelings and thoughts about life in this world and the Next World, and the different judgements of the times of night and day. So through all of that he was aware of his own astonishment and the astonishment of others respecting his shaykh's rectitude, gravity and certainty. Sometimes his Shaykh Ibn Nasir disclosed to him that which was transpiring in himself and he made it clear and explained it to him so that no uncertainty remained about it.

He stated that once when he was sitting before him he was wondering about how the shaykh had earned the wealth which he had used to get married, go on hajj, and buy books when the property of the zawiya was a *waqf* over which he had no right of disposal. Then the Shaykh turned to him and explained for him the normal means of earning and cultivation by which he had earned all of that. That was mentioned in a selection of what has been transmitted from the *Lectures* and *Index* of al-Yusi. As he revealed his actions to him, he explained to him what was right and wrong in them and guided him when he was afraid of him wavering or deviating from the Path. That is how al-Yusi, who was called "the Lightning-Bolt of Knowledges", bowed his head before Shaykh Ibn Nasir out of respect and esteem.

Shaykh Abu Salim al-'Ayyashi (d 1090 AH) said in his book, *The Gift of the Close Friends*, that Shaykh Ibn Nasir, may Allah be pleased with him, was scrupulous about following the Sunna in all his states, even in respect of his clothes and food, and in all forms of worship and daily life. In that he followed the path of other great righteous men such as al-Marjani, Ibn Abi Jamra, and Ibn al-Hajj. He went on hajj and to visit the Prophet twice, and on his journeys he met notable Imams. He transmitted from them and they took knowledge him as well. So his paths of *riwaya* were as extensive as his method in understanding was proficient.

There is no harm here if we digress to something which the *Fihrist* reports. When Imam al-Hasan al-Yusi and his son Muhammad went on hajj in 1098 AH, they did not take anything from the scholars of the Muslim lands where they travelled. It is said that that was because they did not find anyone with more knowledge than them so that they could take from them. One of the desires of the great Maghribi scholars when they go on hajj and to Madina is to meet other scholars in the Muslim lands and take knowledge from them and their reports do not omit any scholar in that.

So we recognise the scholarly position of al-Yusi from the fact that he did not take from anyone in his hajj journey and, therefore, we must, in turn, recognise the position of his shaykh Ibn Nasir before whom al-Yusi was so humble and with whom he studied and boasted of the fact that he was one of his shaykhs and whom he praised in his poem in *dal* which disclose clear divine opening which also appeared in his Nasiri supplication. The *Mashishiyya* prayer says:

If words are in the heart,
the tongue is a guide to what is in the heart.

That refers to the contents of their selves which Allah makes appear on their tongues. If someone contains a secret, Allah makes him wear its cloak.

The person who compiled the selection quotes Abu Salim al-'Ayyashi as saying, "As for *tasawwuf*, he took from his shaykh Sidi 'Abdullah ibn Husayn ar-Raqqi. When his death was near, he left him in the care of his brother in Allah, Sidi Ahmad ibn Ibrahim. When, in turn, his death drew near, he commanded him to care for the madrasa and zawiyya and to marry his widow." That happened.

He himself undertook to teach the sciences of Arabic to his children because he considered their instruction to be part of *'ibada*. He taught the book at-*Tashhil* in grammar by Imam Ibn Malik (d. 672 AH). He had memorised it. It is said that the copy which he read is still extant in the Tamagrut Archives.

Part of the refinement and intelligence of Shaykh Ibn Nasir was that he became aware that the scholar Sidi Muhammad ibn Sa'id as-Susi al-Mirghiti (d. 1089 AH) – who lived in Marrakesh and wrote *al-Muqanna'* on the times of the prayer – had the idea that the people of the Nasiri zawiyya were giving the *adhan* of Maghrib before the time. The zawiyya had a minaret but the *adhan* was often given from a high hill nearby. So Shaykh Ibn Nasir suggested to his guest Sidi Muhammad ibn Sa'id that they climb the minaret at the time of sunset. When they were relaxing in the gathering, Shaykh Ibn Nasir said to his guest, "Perhaps it is the time of Maghrib." Almost as soon as the other said to him, "Yes," the mu'adhdhan of the zawiyya, the uncle of Ahmad ibn 'Abdu'r-Rahman gave the adhan. Shaykh al-Mirghiti used to say after that that the uncle of Ahmad ibn 'Abdu'r-Rahman knew the times of the prayer like he knew his own sons.

Allah gave Shaykh Ibn Nasir to the people of his time and he made the Deen firm in them and revived the Islamic Shari'a through him. The students of the Nasiri zawiyya made journeys and excursions among the tribes of the Sus and all the regions of the south there termed to be part of the people of the *qibla*. It is borders of the desert now. The first of their goals was to guide people and to found schools, mosques and Nasiri zawiyyas where there was devotion to *'ibada* and *dhikr*, especially the prayer on the Prophet, may Allah bless him and grant him peace, on Thursday nights and Friday mornings. The people were intent on doing them in the thousands. That included all circles, including groups of blind men who occupied themselves with it from the morning prayer until the time of Duha. The prayer they used was: "*Allahumma, salli 'ala Sayyidina Muhammad wa 'ala alihi wa sahbihi wa sallam.*" The *baraka* of that appeared in that land in the abundance of water and the spread of inhabitation and crops.

He did not confine himself, may Allah be pleased with him, to establishing *zawiyyas* in the Sus region. Indeed, his area of influence included the centre and the west, Marrakesh, Casablanca, Settat, Ribat, Sale and Fes. And it was his *zawiyya* in Fes which became the fountainhead of national awakening which was the reason for the liberation of the entire Maghrib from French colonialism. The scholar Sidi Muhammad Ghazi al-Maknasi, who was the first Maghribi ambassador to Saudi Arabia, used to go there and used it as a free madrasa. His brothers among the noble students of the Qarawiyyin went there, and they used to meet them to study and discuss and we do not need to pursue this.

Shaykh Ibn Nasir instituted a *hizb* in the Sus region known as the "Hizb of the Shaykh" which is attributed to him, may Allah be pleased with him. It is the famous *hizb* which is recited in a group morning and evening in many mosques, although this shaykh used to cancel the *hizb* on Thursday nights and replace it with Surat al-Kahf since there is a sound hadith that if anyone recites this sura on Thursday night, Allah will preserve him until the end of the week. He also cancelled the Friday morning *hizb* and replaced it with Surat Yasin, ad-Dukhan, al-Waqi'a, al-Mulk, al-Insan, al-Buruj and about five thousand prayers on the Prophet, may Allah bless him and grant him peace. This was for the students involved in teaching and learning. As for the fuqara' and the murids, sometimes they did ten or twenty thousand prayers on the Prophet on Friday night and morning. Those replaced *hizbs* exceeded the period of a normal month and so the whole Qur'an was completed in about 35 days. In this way the conclusion of the Qur'an always coincided with a Sunday night and always began on Monday morning. That was to take advantage of the benefits of the sound hadiths and what the Shaykh saw of the *baraka* entailed in reciting of those suras at those times. Would that this *hizb* had spread everywhere!

Credit goes to Shaykh Ibn Nasir and his students for what we can see to this day of clear religious commitment in all the rural areas of the Sus. He also has the credit for heating the *wudu'* water in all the mosques in the towns and desert.

His Sufi tariqa is a branch, like the Darqawi tariqa, of the Shadhiliya tariqa which was founded by the Qutb Abu'l-Hasan 'Ali ibn 'Abdullah al-Ghamari ash-Shadhili (d. 656 AH at 'Aydhab in Egypt). Shaykh Ibn Nasir took the Nasiri tariqa from his shaykh, Sidi 'Abdullah ibn Husayn, who had it from Sidi Ahmad ibn 'Ali al-Hajji from Abu'l-Qasim al-Ghazi from Sidi 'Ali ibn 'Abdullah as-Sijalmasi from Shaykh Ahmad ibn Yusuf ar-Rashidi from Shaykh Abu'l-'Abbas Ahmad Zarruq (d. 899). As for the chain of Shaykh Sidi Zarruq to Abu'l-Hasan ash-Shadhili, it is well-known. It is that shaykh Zarruq took from Sidi Ahmad ibn 'Uqba, who took from Shaykh Yahya ibn Ahmad al-Qadiri from Sidi 'Ali ibn Wafa from his father Sidi Muhammad Wafa from Shaykh Da'ud al-Bakhili from Shaykh Taju'ddin ibn 'Ata'llah al-Iskandari and Shaykh Yaqut al-'Arshi from Sidi Ahmad ibn 'Umar al-Mursi, the khalifa of Abu'l-Hasan ash-Shadhili from him from the Qutb, 'Abdu's-Salam ibn Mashish, and so forth.

Whoever wants more details on the biography of Shaykh Ibn Nasir should Consult the *Index* of al-Yusi and his *Muhadarat*, *Nashr al-Mathani*, which is about the people of the 11th and 12th centuries by Sidi Muhammad ibn at-Tayyib al-Qadiri, and as-Safwa, on the reports of the righteous men of the 11th century by Sidi Muhammad as-Saghir al-Ifrani al-Marakkushi, the middle of the first part of *Salwa al-Anfas* by Sidi Muhammad ibn Ja'far al-Kittani, and *The Inlaid Perals on the Righteous Men of Draa* by Muhammad ibn Musa ibn Nasir (1179 AH).

Shaykh Muhammad ibn Nasir, may Allah be pleased with him, died in 1085 AH and was succeeded by good descendants whose excellence had appeared during his lifetime. That was due to the excellence of his good guidance and exemplary teaching. Sidi Muhammad, his eldest son who died in 1126, was a great scholar, as was his brother Sidi Ahmad, son of the Shaykh, who died in 1129. He succeeded his father in taking charge of the zawiyya by teaching and instructing dhikr through his appointment. He was the author of a popular "Nasiri Hijazi Journey" like Imam al-Yusi, Imam 'Abdu'l-Malik at-Tajmu'ti (d. 1118), Sidi Husaynibn Muhammad ash-Sharhabili, the student of Sidi Ahmad, the son of the Shaykh, (d, 1152), and Imam Sidi Muhammad ibn 'Abdu's-Salam ibn 'Abdullah ibn Muhammad al-Kabir ibn Shaykh Ibn Nasir, (d. 1239). He was the author of another Hijazi journey which is full of lessons in knowledge.

As for the qasida of Imam al-Yusi in which he praised his shaykh Ibn Nasir when he returned from one of his hajjs, Sidi Muhammad ibn Ja'far al-Kittani mentions it on page 264, part one of *as-Salwa* when he deals with Shaykh Ibn Nasir:

> Important imams like the scholar al-Yusi studied with him. He praised him in his famous and unrivalled poem in *dal* which the people of literature compare to the poem in *dal* by al-Busiri in praise of Abu'l-Hasan ash-Shadhili and Abu'l-'Abbas al-Mursi. It has 300 verses and he wrote an excellent commentary on it. It is not easy to imagine anyone getting the better of Imam al-Yusi were it not for the esteem he himself held for the position of the shaykh.

The Susis divided it over the days of the week, and they used to recite a part of it with the regular hizb every evening as they do with the *Burda* of al-Busiri in the evening and his poem in *hamza* in the morning. There are none of his students who have not memorised these three poems by listening to them when regularly attending the recitation of the *hizb*. It begins:

He ascended the rosy mountains
   between al-Lasab and Dhat al-Armad
Across from al-Jar' which is in the lowlands
   are the graves of the men of the Hammad tribe.

There is an excerpt from it which praises the shaykh in which he says:

The Succour of people, Shaykh Ibn Nasir
   by whom Allah helped the Shari'a of Ahmad.
He restored the radiant face of the Deen
   and the radiance of the source of every unifier.
He established the roof of its structure which is above
   all roofs over the unshakeable warners.
He removed doubt from every dark night
   as well as misguidance, error and harshness.

Then he says to him:

Congratulations on the glory which is unsurpassed in time
   from a hopeful riser and ascender
Congratulations on the treasure which was obtained before

by the paragons of the ascetic gnostics.
When such a treasure is obtained, youth ceases
and does not need any increase or provision.
Say to the one who tries that he has fallen short
because he tried to hold the Pleaides in his hand.

He ends it with his words:

The nights delight and enjoy your blaze
and the one connected to those who possess happiness is happy.

As for his supplication whose *baraka* we hope for in this preface, it is an indication of his state and the form of his thought. The adage goes: "They speak and are known." In it he directed himself to the way that a truthful Muslim must constantly put his trust in Allah and turn to him in hardships and matters of concern while maintaining the good *adab* of a slave and being humble to his Lord, since that is one of the things which will bring about the response. All of that is expressed in strong firm expressions while at the same time it is simple and sweet in its order. This indicates that its author is conversant with lofty adab. Its expression is such that the listener supposes he may be able to come up with something similar but is then unable to achieve that, as so often happens with deceptive simplicity.

Look and see how he begins it by asking for the help of the One to Whose mercy the people of hardships and mishaps flee. That is Allah Almighty. He encompassed that flight by the mercy of Allah by preceding it with the '*jarr wa majrur*' (preposition and its complement) to which they connected. It is known that putting the objective first proclaims its containment. This is like the words of the Almighty, "*You only we worship and You only we ask for help.*" So it is as if he were saying, "O You to whose mercy is the only possible flight from concerns and hardships!"

Then he follows that with calling on the only One who can provide deliverance and protection for the concerned and in need, and the One who is the only source of refuge from things which are feared. When one is constricted, there is no one but Him who can be sought as a deliverer or reliever. It is well-known that when someone in dire need calls upon Allah, He removes from him what troubles him. Allah Almighty says, "*He who responds to the oppressed when they call to Him and removes their distress.*" (27:62)

This is like what he said with elegant sweet words:

O You to whose mercy one flees!
You in whom the one in need and distress seeks refuge!

This verse alone embraces the meaning of the whole *qasida* and acts as a summary for it. If the one compelled devotes himself to Allah alone, he repeatedly calls on Him truthfully and sincerely after the answer because Allah has no need of hearing of the details. His knowledge of the state dispenses with the need for asking.

All the verses of the supplication are an example of excellent arrangement and a deep expression of complete trust in Allah Almighty. We see him praying for things in the Next World as he prayers for affairs in this world, and he proclaims that the Next World is the final destination in any case and that it is better than this one. He says:

O Lord, make it our habit to cling and devote ourselves
to the resplendent Sunna.
Confine our manifold desires to You
and grant us full and complete gnosis.
Combine both knowledge and action for us,
and direct our hopes to the Abiding Abode.

This supplication has been tried, tested and proven to relieve distress and to avert difficult situations, especially when they are societal and concern the affairs of all the Muslims. The people of Fez call it "The Sword of Ibn Nasir". They used to teach it to the pupils in the Qur'anic *kuttabs* and they used it to seek refuge with Allah, using various tunes, in the time of the French oppression and occupation of Morocco. That is the custom of the Muslims: to seek refuge with Allah Almighty in times of hardship. Your Lord says, "*Call on Me and I will answer you.*" (40:60)

We ask Allah Almighty to make our end and the ends of the Muslims good and to place us on the path of the best of the Salaf of the Muslim Community and to fill our hearts with what pleases Him and to be kind to us in all states. Peace.

Ribat 1399/1979
Muhammad ibn 'Abdullah ar-Radani

بسم الله الرحمن الرحيم
وصلى الله على سيدنا محمد وآله

يَا مَنْ إِلَى رَحْمَتِهِ الْمَفَرُّ
وَمَنْ إِلَيْهِ يَلْجَأُ الْمُضْطَرُّ

O You to Whose mercy one flees!

You in Whom the one in need and distress seeks refuge!

وَيَا قَرِيبَ الْعَفْوِ يَا مَوْلَاهُ
وَيَا مُغِيثَ كُلِّ مَنْ دَعَاهُ

O Master, You Whose pardon is near! O my Master!

O You Who help all who call on Him!

بِكَ اسْتَغَثْنَا يَا مُغِيثَ الضُّعَفَا
فَحَسْبُنَا يَا رَبِّ أَنْتَ وَكَفَى

We seek Your help, O You who help the weak!

You are enough for us, O Lord!

فَلاَ أَجَلَّ مِنْ عَظِيمِ قُدْرَتِكْ
وَلاَ أَعَزَّ مِنْ عَزِيزِ سَطْوَتِكْ

There is nothing more majestic than Your immense power
and nothing mightier than the might of Your force.

لِعِزِّ مُلْكِكَ الْمُلُوكُ تَخْضَعُ
تَخْفِضُ قَدْرَ مَنْ تَشَا وَتَرْفَعُ

Kings are humbled to the might of Your domain
and You lower or elevate whomever You wish.

وَالْأَمْرُ كُلُّهُ إِلَيْكَ رَدُّهُ
وَبِيَدَيْكَ حَلُّهُ وَعَقْدُهُ

The entire affair returns to You,
and the release or conclusion of all matters is in Your hand.

وَقَدْ رَفَعْنَا أَمْرَنَا إِلَيْكَ
وَقَدْ شَكَوْنَا ضُعْفَنَا عَلَيْكَ

We have presented our affair before You,
and we complain to You of our weakness.

فَارْحَمْنَا يَا مَنْ لَاَّ يَزَالُ عَالِمًا
بِضُعْفِنَا وَلَا يَزَالُ رَاحِمًا

Have mercy on us, O You Who know our weakness
and Who continues to be merciful.

اُنْظُرْ إِلَى مَا مَسَّنَا مِنَ الْوَرَى
فَحَالُنَا مِنْ بَيْنِهِمْ كَمَا تَرَى

Look at what we have experienced from people!
Our state among them is as You see.

قَدْ قَلَّ جَمْعُنَا وَقَلَّ وَفْرُنَا
وَانْحَطَّ مَا بَيْنَ الْجُمُوعِ قَدْرُنَا

Our troops are few and our wealth is little.
Our power has declined among groups.

وَاسْتَضْعَفُونَا شَوْكَةً وَشِدَّةْ
وَاسْتَنْقَصُونَا عُدَّةً وَعِدَّةْ

They have weakened our solidarity and strength
and diminished our numbers and our preparation.

فَنَحْنُ يَا مَنْ مُلْكُهُ لاَ يُسْلَبُ
لُذْنَا بِجَاهِكَ الَّذِي لاَ يُغْلَبُ

O You Whose kingdom cannot be pillaged,
give us shelter by Your rank which is never overcome!

إِلَيْكَ يَاغَوْثَ الْفَقِيرِ نَسْتَنِدْ
عَلَيْكَ يَا كَهْفَ الضَّعِيفِ نَعْتَمِدْ

O Succour of the poor, we trust in You!
O Cave of the weak, we rely on You!

أَنْتَ الَّذِي نَدْعُو لِكَشْفِ الْغَمَرَاتْ
أَنْتَ الَّذِي نَرْجُو لِدَفْعِ الْحَسَرَاتْ

You are the One on Whom We call to remove adversities,
and You are the One we hope will dispel our sorrows.

أَنْتَ الْعِنَايَةُ الَّتِي لاَ نَرْتَجِي
حِمَايَةً مِنْ غَيْرِ بَابِهَا تَجِي

You have such concern for us that we cannot hope
for protection which comes through any other door.

أَنْتَ الَّذِي نَسْعَى بِبَابِ فَضْلِهِ
أَكْرَمُ مَنْ أَغْنَى بِفَيْضِ نَيْلِهِ

We strive to reach the door of Your bounty

Most Generous of those who enrich by the super-abundance of their favour.

أَنْتَ الَّذِي تَهْدِي إِذَا ضَلَلْنَا
أَنْتَ الَّذِي تَعْفُو إِذَا زَلَلْنَا

You are the One Who guides when we are misguided.

You are the One who pardons when we slip.

وَسِعْتَ كُلَّ مَا خَلَقْتَ عِلْمَا
وَرَأْفَةً وَرَحْمَةً وَحِلْمَا

You have full knowledge of all You have created

and encompassing compassion, mercy and forbearance.

وَلَيْسَ مِنَّا فِي الْوُجُودِ أَحْقَرُ
وَلاَ لِمَا عِنْدَكَ مِنَّا أَفْقَرُ

There is no one in existence more lowly than we are

nor poorer and more in need of what You have than us.

يَا وَاسِعَ الإِحْسَانِ يَامَنْ خَيْرُهُ
عَمَّ الْوَرَى وَلاَ يُنَادَى غَيْرُهُ

O you of vast kindness! O You Whose good encompasses all mankind, and no other is called on!

يَا مُنْقِذَ الْغَرْقَى وَيَا حَنَّانُ
يَا مُنْجِيَ الْهَلْكَى وَيَا مَنَّانُ

O Saviour of the drowning! O Compassionate!
O rescuer of the lost! O Gracious Bestower!

ضَاقَ النِّطَاقُ يَا سَمِيعُ يَا مُجِيبْ
عَزَّ الدَّوَاءُ يَا سَرِيعُ يَا قَرِيبْ

Words are lacking, O Hearing, O Answerer!
The cure is difficult, O Swift! O Near!

وَقَدْ مَدَدْنَا رَبَّنَا الأَكُفَّ
وَمِنْكَ رَبَّنَا رَجَوْنَا اللُّطْفَ

To you, our Lord, we have stretched out our hands
and from You, our Lord, we hope for kindness.

فَالْطُفْ بِنَا فِيمَا بِهِ قَضَيْتَ
وَرَضِّنَا بِمَا بِهِ رَضِيتَ

Be kind to us in what You decree
and let us be pleased with what pleases You.

وَأَبْدِلِ اللَّهُمَّ حَالَ الْعُسْرِ
بِالْيُسْرِ وَامْدُدْنَا بِرِيحِ النَّصْرِ

O Allah, change the state of hardship
for ease and help us with the wind of victory.

وَاجْعَلْ لَنَا عَلَى الْبُغَاةِ الْغَلَبَةْ
وَاقْصُرْ أَذَى الشَّرِّ عَلَى مَنْ طَلَبَهْ

Give us victory over the aggressors
and contain the evil among those who asked for it.

وَاقْهَرْ عِدَانَا يَا عَزِيزُ قَهْرَا
يَفْصِمُ حَبْلَهُمْ وَيُصْمِي الظَّهْرَا

Overpower our enemy, O Mighty, with a force
which disorders them and crushes them.

وَاعْكِسْ مُرَادَهُمْ وَخَيِّبْ سَعْيَهُمْ

وَاهْزِمْ جُيُوشَهُمْ وَأَفْسِدْ رَأْيَهُمْ

Overturn what they desire and make their efforts fail,

defeat their armies and unsettle their resolve.

وَعَجِّلِ اللَّهُمَّ فِيهِمْ نِقْمَتَكْ

فَإِنَّهُمْ لاَ يُعْجِزُونَ قُدْرَتَكْ

O Allah, hasten Your revenge among them

They cannot stand before Your power.

يَا رَبِّ يَا رَبِّ بِحَبْلِ عِصْمَتِكْ

قَدِ اعْتَصَمْنَا وَبِعِزِّ نُصْرَتِكْ

O Lord, O Lord, Our protection is by Your love,

and by the might of Your help.

فَكُنْ لَنَا وَلاَ تَكُنْ عَلَيْنَا

وَلاَ تَكِلْنَا طَرْفَةً إِلَيْنَا

Be for us and do not be against us.

Do not leave us to ourselves for a single instant.

فَمَا أَطَقْنَا قُوَّةً لِلدَّفْعِ

وَلاَ اسْتَطَعْنَا حِيلَةً لِلنَّفْعِ

We have no power of defence

nor have we any device to bring about our benefit.

وَمَا قَصَدْنَا غَيْرَ بَابِكَ الْكَرِيمْ

وَمَا رَجَوْنَا غَيْرَ فَضْلِكَ الْعَمِيمْ

We do not aim for other than Your noble door,

and we do not hope for other than Your encompassing bounty.

فَمَا رَجَتْ مِنْ خَيْرِكَ الظُّنُونُ

بِنَفْسِ مَا تَقُولُ كُنْ يَكُونُ

Minds only hope for Your blessing

by the simple fact that you say 'Be" and it is.

يَا رَبِّ يَا رَبِّ بِكَ التَّوَصُّلُ

لِمَا لَدَيْكَ وَبِكَ التَّوَسُّلُ

O Lord, O Lord, arrival is by You

to what You have and seeking the means is by You!

يَا رَبِّ أَنْتَ رُكْنُنَا الرَّفِيعُ

يَا رَبِّ أَنْتَ حِصْنُنَا الْمَنِيعُ

O Lord, You are our high pillar of support!

O Lord, You are our impregnable fortress.

يَا رَبِّ يَا رَبِّ أَنِلْنَا الأَمْنَا

إِذَا ارْتَحَلْنَا وَإِذَا أَقَمْنَا

O Lord, O Lord, give us security

when we travel and when we remain.

يَا رَبِّ وَاحْفَظْ زَرْعَنَا وَضَرْعَنَا

وَاحْفَظْ تِجَارَنَا وَوَفِّرْ جَمْعَنَا

O Lord, preserve our crops and herds,

and preserve our trade and make our numbers more!

وَاجْعَلْ بِلاَدَنَا بِلاَدَ الدِّينِ

وَرَاحَةَ الْمُحْتَاجِ وَالْمِسْكِينِ

Make our land a land of the deen

and repose for the needy and the poor.

وَاجْعَلْ لَهَا بَيْنَ الْبِلَادِ صَوْلَةً

وَحُرْمَةً وَمَنْعَةً وَدَوْلَةً

Give us force among the lands as well as respect,

impregnability and a polity.

وَاجْعَلْ مِنَ السِّرِّ الْمَصُونِ عِزَّهَا

وَاجْعَلْ مِنَ السِّتْرِ الْجَمِيلِ حِرْزِهَا

Appoint it its might from the protected secret,

and grant it protection by the beautiful veiling

وَاجْعَلْ بِصَادٍ وَبِقَافٍ وَبِنُونْ

أَلْفَ حِجَابٍ مِنْ وَرَائِهَا يَكُونْ

By sad, qaf and nun,

place a thousand veils in front of it.

بِجَاهِ نُورِ وَجْهِكَ الْكَرِيمِ

وَجَاهِ سِرِّ مُلْكِكَ الْعَظِيمِ

By the rank of the light of Your noble Face

and the rank of the secret of Your immense kingdom,

وَجَاهِ لاَ إِلَهَ إِلاَّ اللَّهُ

وَجَاهِ خَيْرِ الْخَلْقِ يَا رَبَّاهُ

And the rank of 'la ilaha illa'llah'

and the rank of the Best of Creation, O our Lord,

وَجَاهِ مَا بِهِ دَعَاكَ الأَنْبِيَاءْ

وَجَاهِ مَا بِهِ دَعَاكَ الأَوْلِيَاءْ

And the rank of that by which the Prophets prayed to You

and the rank of that by which the Awliya' pray to you,

وَجَاهِ قَدْرِ الْقُطْبِ وَالأَوْتَادِ

وَجَاهِ حَالِ الْجَرْسِ وَالأَفْرَادِ

And the rank of the power of the Qutb and the Awtad

and the rank of the Jaras and Afrad,

وَجَاهِ الأَخْيَارِ وَجَاهِ النُّجَبَا

وَجَاهِ الأَبْدَالِ وَجَاهِ النُّقَبَا

And the rank of the Akhyar and the rank of Nujaba'

and the rank of the Abdal and the rank of the Nuqaba',

وَجَاهِ كُلِّ عَابِدٍ وَذَاكِرْ
وَجَاهِ كُلِّ حَامِدٍ وَشَاكِرْ

And the rank of every one worshipping and doing dhikr

and the rank of everyone praising and giving thanks,

وَجَاهِ كُلِّ مَنْ رَفَعْتَ قَدْرَهُ
مِمَّنْ سَتَرْتَ أَوْ نَشَرْتَ ذِكْرَهُ

And the rank of everyone whose worth You elevated

both those who are concealed and those whose renown has spread,

وَجَاهِ آيَاتِ الْكِتَابِ الْمُحْكَمِ
وَجَاهِ الإِسْمِ الأَعْظَمِ الْمُعَظَّمِ

And the ranks of the firm ayats of the Book

and the rank of the Greatest Supreme Name,

يَا رَبِّ يَا رَبِّ وَقَفْنَا فُقَرَا
بَيْنَ يَدَيْكَ ضُعَفَاءَ حُقَرَا

O Lord, O Lord, we stand as fuqara'

before You, weak and lowly.

وَقَدْ دَعَوْنَاكَ دُعَاءَ مَنْ دَعَا
رَبّاً كَرِيمًا لاَ يَرُدُّ مَنْ سَعَى

We called to You with the supplication of the one who calls
on a noble Lord who does not reject those who strive.

فَاقْبَلْ دُعَاءَنَا بِمَحْضِ الْفَضْلِ
قَبُولَ مَنْ أَلْغَى حِسَابَ الْعَدْلِ

Accept our supplication by pure grace,

with the acceptance of someone who sets aside the fair reckoning.

وَامْنُنْ عَلَيْنَا مِنَّةَ الْكَرِيمِ
وَاعْطِفْ عَلَيْنَا عَطْفَةَ الْحَلِيمِ

Bestow on us the favour of the Generous,

and show us the kindness of the Forbearing.

وَانْشُرْ عَلَيْنَا يَا رَحِيمُ رَحْمَتَكْ
وَبْسُطْ عَلَيْنَا يَا كَرِيمُ نِعْمَتَكْ

O Merciful, extend Your mercy over us

and spread Your blessing over us, O Generous.

وَخِرْ لَنَا فِي سَائِرِ الأَقْوَالِ
وَاخْتَرْ لَنَا فِي سَائِرِ الأَفْعَالِ

Choose for us in all our words
and select for us in all our actions.

يَا رَبِّ وَاجْعَلْ دَأْبَنَا التَّمَسُّكَا
بِالسُّنَّةِ الْغَرَّاءِ وَالتَّنَسُّكَا

O Lord, make it our habit to cling and devote ourselves
to the resplendent Sunna.

وَاحْصُرْ لَنَا أَغْرَاضَنَا الْمُخْتَلِفَةْ
فِيكَ وَعَرِّفْنَا تَمَامَ الْمَعْرِفَةْ

Confine our manifold desires to You
and grant us full and complete gnosis.

وَاجْمَعْ لَنَا مَا بَيْنَ عِلْمٍ وَعَمَلْ
وَاصْرِفْ إِلَى دَارِ الْبَقَا مِنَّا الأَمَلْ

Combine both knowledge and action for us,
and direct our hopes to the Abiding Abode.

وَانْهَجْ بِنَا يَا رَبِّ نَهْجَ السُّعَدَا

وَاخْتِمْ لَنَا يَا رَبِّ خَتْمَ الشُّهَدَا

O Lord, make us follow the road of the fortunate

and make our seal the Seal of the martyrs, O Lord!

وَاجْعَلْ بَنِينَا فُضَلَاءَ صُلَحَا

وَعُلَمَاءَ عَامِلِينَ نُصَحَا

Make our sons virtuous and righteous,

scholars with action and people of good counsel.

وَأَصْلِحِ اللَّهُمَّ حَالَ الأَهْلِ

وَيَسِّرِ اللَّهُمَّ جَمْعَ الشَّمْلِ

O Allah, remedy the situation of the people

and, O Allah, make the reunification easy.

يَا رَبِّ وَافْتَحْ فَتْحَكَ الْمُبِينَ

لِمَنْ تَوَلَّى وَأَعَزَّ الدِّينَ

O Lord, grant Your clear victory to the one

who takes charge and empowers the Deen,

وَانْصُرْهُ يَا ذَا الطَّوْلِ وَانْصُرْ حِزْبَهُ
وَامْلأْ بِمَا يُرْضِيكَ عَنْهُ قَلْبَهُ

And help him, O You Who are forbearing, and help his party and fill his heart with what will make him pleasing to you.

يَا رَبِّ وَانْصُرْ دِينَنَا الْمُحَمَّدِي
وَاجْعَلْ خِتَامَ عِزِّهِ كَمَا بُدِي

O Lord, help our Muhammadan deen,
and make it end mighty as it began.

وَاحْفَظْهُ يَا رَبِّ بِحِفْظِ الْعُلَمَا
وَارْفَعْ مَنَارَ نُورِهِ إِلَى السَّمَا

Preserve it, O Lord, through the preservation of the scholars,
and raise the minaret of its light to heaven.

وَاعْفُ وَعَافِ وَاكْفِ وَاغْفِرْ ذَنْبَنَا
وَذَنْبَ كُلِّ مُسْلِمٍ يَا رَبَّنَا

Pardon, grant well-being, make up for our deficiency
and forgive our sins and the sins of every Muslim, O our Lord.

وَ صَلِّ يَا رَبِّ عَلَى الْمُخْتَارِ
صَلاَتَكَ الْكَامِلَةَ الْمِقْدَارِ

O Lord, bless the Chosen one
with your perfect prayer of blessing.

صَلاَتَكَ الَّتِي تَفِي بِأَمْرِهِ
كَمَا يَلِيقُ بِارْتِفَاعِ قَدْرِهِ

Your prayer is that which grant success in his business
as befits his lofty worth.

ثُمَّ عَلَى الآلِ الْكِرَامِ وَعَلَى
أَصْحَابِهِ الْغُرِّ وَمَنْ لَهُمْ تَلاَ

Then bless his noble family and glorious Companions
and those who have followed them.

وَالْحَمْدُ لِلَّهِ الَّذِي بِحَمْدِهِ
يَبْلُغُ ذُو الْقَصْدِ تَمَامَ قَصْدِهِ

Praise belongs to Allah by whose praise
those with an aim completely fulfil that aim.

www.ingramcontent.com/pod-product-compliance
Lightning Source LLC
Chambersburg PA
CBHW060647030426
42337CB00018B/3490
9781908892454